be mine

YOU MAKE ME SMILE

be mine

25 PAPER PROJECTS TO SHARE THE LOVE

SALLY J SHIM

PHOTOGRAPHS BY MAX WANGER

CHRONICLE BOOKS

SAN FRANCISCO

Text copyright © 2015 by Sally J Shim
Photographs © 2015 by Chronicle Books LLC

Library of Congress Cataloging-in-Publication Data:

Shim, Sally J.
  Be mine : 25 paper projects to share the love / Sally J Shim ; Photographs by Max Wanger.
    pages cm
  Summary: "This paper-crafting book presents 25 projects including handmade cards and
party favors that can be gifted and enjoyed any time of year"—Provided by publisher.
  ISBN 978-1-4521-4186-2 (paperback)
  1. Paper work. 2. Greeting cards. I. Title.

  TT870.S4525 2015
  745.594'1—dc23

                    2015021149

Manufactured in China

FSC
www.fsc.org
MIX
Paper from
responsible sources
FSC™ C104723

Design by Anne Kenady
Photographs by Max Wanger

EK Tools is a registered trademark of EK Success Ltd. Scotch Adhesive Transfer Tape,
Scotch Quick-Drying Tacky Glue, and Scotch Wrinkle-Free Glue Stick are registered
trademarks of 3M Company. X-ACTO knife is a registered trademark of Elmer's
Products, Inc. Xyron Sticker Maker is a registered trademark of Xyron, Inc.

10 9 8 7 6 5 4 3 2 1

Chronicle Books LLC
680 Second Street
San Francisco, California 94107
www.chroniclebooks.com

contents

INTRODUCTION

There are few things more wonderful than the joy that comes from being with good friends and family. Despite how much we appreciate the special people in our life, we don't often take the time to express it. Sending a heartfelt message—or a love greeting—to a friend or loved one is a meaningful way to show that you cherish their presence in your life.

In these days of high-speed communication, finding the time to hand-make a special love greeting may not always seem workable but it's well worth it. Taking time out of our busy schedules to sit down and focus on making something requires patience and dedication, but the result can be priceless. The maker will have enjoyed the creative process—which often leads to more creative projects—and the recipient will be delighted with the gift of a handmade greeting.

Love greetings are not meant solely for Valentine's Day or anniversaries. In fact, they can be everyday reminders of your affection for a loved one in your life. Many of the projects in this book were designed for everyday giving and can also be used for memorable occasions like birthdays and weddings. Whether for your spouse, partner, parent, sibling, child, or friend, expressing your love and appreciation is a beautiful gesture.

To hold a handmade greeting is to appreciate the effort invested in making it. The recipient will not only recognize the beauty of the final creation but will also reflect on the maker's intention and the time spent on the item. I have been making handmade cards and gifts for years, and the response from the recipient is always the same—true gratitude.

This book is filled with simple and sweet love greetings that are perfect for all skill levels. If you are a beginner and have never picked up an X-ACTO knife, don't fret; this book is for you. And if you are a seasoned crafter and have a studio stocked with amazing paper and craft supplies, this book is also for you. Most of the projects require only a few basic materials and tools and can be completed in a short amount of time. More than half of the projects in the book utilize design elements called printables (see Printables, page 24). The printables can be reproduced from your home computer and printer and will enable you to create love greetings identical to what you see in the project photograph. Each project also suggests a few variations for each item, making it simple for you to create a distinctive love greeting and encouraging you to think outside the box.

It is my hope that this book will inspire you to share your love in a new way—by creating handmade love greetings for the special people in your life!

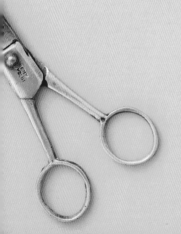

materials
& tools

In my studio, I store a well-curated supply of paper and craft materials that enables me to make handmade cards, greetings, and gifts at any time. Stock up on the materials and tools in the following lists and enjoy making not only the projects in this book but whatever paper project you can imagine. ♥

materials

While paper is often the star of any paper-crafting project, a vast range of other materials will help you achieve special effects and customized touches. The listed materials are paper-crafting basics (such as paper, envelopes, and decorative binding) as well as miscellaneous other materials used in the projects in this book.

paper

One of the most fun aspects of paper crafting is the paper itself. Inexpensive and available in a wide selection of textures, patterns, thicknesses, and colors, paper is an ideal material for creative expression—and for sharing your love! The projects in this book call for many different types of paper, inviting you to seek out kinds you've never used before or do new things with papers you already enjoy working with. Here is a list of the papers you'll encounter in the projects in this book. Note: Store paper in a cool, dry, dark space to prevent it from curling or fading.

CARDSTOCK

Cardstock is a heavyweight paper that is ideal for making greeting cards and boxes.

Scrapbook paper, catalog covers, and business cards are examples of types of cardstock.

CREPE PAPER

Crepe paper is a durable, crinkled tissue paper. It can stretch widthwise, making it ideal for making paper flowers.

GLITTER PAPER

Glitter paper has the thickness of cardstock and is covered on one side with glitter.

KRAFT PAPER

Kraft paper is a sturdy paper made from wood pulp. It comes in a variety of thicknesses and tan-colored shades and is sold in rolls or in sheets. Butcher paper is a type of kraft paper.

ORIGAMI PAPER

Origami paper is a lightweight paper used in the craft of Japanese origami paper folding. It is also highly adaptable to many paper crafts. Sold in square sheets, it comes in a dazzling range of colors and patterns.

PARCHMENT PAPER

Parchment paper, often used by bakers, features a nonstick surface. It can be cut to size and also serves as a helpful work surface for projects using polymer clay.

RICE PAPER

Rice paper is a thin, textured paper that is not made from rice but is derived from the pith of the rice paper plant. The paper is traditionally used in Asia for painting. Rice paper is often dyed a variety of colors.

STICKER PAPER

Sticker paper is matte paper with one adhesive side covered by a backing that peels off. With sticker paper, you can create labels, stickers, or adhesive patterned paper. It comes in many colors.

TEXT-WEIGHT PAPER

Text-weight paper is a lightweight paper that is easy to cut and fold. It comes in a variety of colors and textures. Note: Standard copy paper can be used for projects that call for white text-weight paper.

VELLUM PAPER

Vellum paper is a medium-weight paper that is translucent. It comes in many colors.

WOOD VENEER PAPER

Wood veneer paper is a thin sheet of wood backed with paper. It is available in different sizes and wood types. Wood veneer paper can be found at paper supply and woodworking stores.

envelopes and bags

Envelopes and bags can be used not only for packaging cards and small items but also as elements of a love greeting design. Here are a few basic types that can be incorporated into paper-crafting projects.

CLEAR SELF-SEALING ENVELOPES

Clear self-sealing envelopes are made of a transparent, plastic-like material and feature an adhesive closure that is covered with a peel-off strip.

GLASSINE BAGS

Glassine bags are made of thin, translucent, water-resistant paper.

PAPER ENVELOPES

Paper envelopes are most commonly used for mailing cards and letters but can be used to contain lots of kinds of items.

decorative binding

Decorative binding is a strip of material woven from natural or synthetic fibers and comes in an endless array of colors, patterns, and textures. It is used to enclose raw edges of materials or items, to secure items together, or just for decorative purposes. It can add a special finishing touch to a love greeting. Note: Store decorative binding on spools or in separate bags to prevent it from being tangled.

RIBBON

Ribbons come in countless materials and textures, such as grosgrain, satin, silk, and linen, and can be purchased by the spool or in smaller quantities at fabric or notions shops. Cloth ribbon is ideal for tying around gifts and making bows.

STRING

String is composed of twisted threads of cotton or other material. Types of string include yarn, embroidery thread, and sewing thread, which are found on spools or in small skeins at fabric or craft stores.

TWILL TAPE

Twill tape is a flat woven ribbon made from cotton or linen that easily absorbs dye or paint. Twill tape can be used for tying bows on packages. It can be found at fabric stores in many widths, textures, and colors.

TWINE

Twine is a durable form of string. Types of twine include baker's twine, jute, sisal, cotton, and flax—all of which can be used when a project in this book calls for twine (unless a type is specified). Twine comes in different materials, even glitter!

miscellaneous materials

The projects in this book call for a selection of unexpected materials (listed ahead) that will make your handmade love greetings truly unique. Most of them can be found at art supply stores and craft stores. Thanks to the versatility of these materials, you will find yourself using them not only to make the love greetings in this book but also in future craft projects.

BALLOONS

Balloons are delightful even when they're not inflated and can offer unexpected texture to a love greeting.

BEAD WITH HOLE

A bead is a small decorative object made from a variety of materials; it comes in different shapes, colors, and sizes. Beads come with a hole through the center and can be threaded onto string, thread, or wire. They can be strung together in a long chain or sewn individually to other objects.

BRADS

A brad is a metal fastener with bendable extensions used to join together pieces of paper.

CARDBOARD MAILING TUBE

A cardboard mailing tube, which is typically used for mailing and shipping purposes, has a cap on both ends that seals the tube closed. It can be used as a container in craft projects.

FELT

Felt is a textile made from natural or synthetic fibers that have been matted and condensed together. Common types of felt are made from wool or acrylic or a blend of both. Felt is easy to cut into shapes, and the edges do not fray, making the material perfect for craft projects.

FLORAL STEM WIRE

Floral stem wire is used for making or stabilizing flower stems. It is usually green and comes in various gauges (thicknesses) and lengths.

GLASS BOTTLE WITH CORK TOP

A glass bottle with a cork top can be used as a love-themed decorative container.

IRON-ON LETTERS

Iron-on letters can be permanently affixed to fabric using a dry iron, offering creative ways to incorporate messages into your love greeting. They come in many materials, including soft-flocked.

LETTER STICKERS

Self-adhesive letter stickers can be used to spell out the words in your love greeting.

METAL EYELET

A metal eyelet is a small metal ring used to reinforce a punched-out hole in materials like fabric, leather, or paper.

PAPER STRAWS

Paper straws, used for drinking beverages, can also be used in paper projects, like for the handle of a paper pinwheel. They come in a wide range of colors, patterns, and diameters.

POLYMER CLAY

Polymer clay is a type of modeling clay that is easy to shape and hardens when heated in the oven.

SEWING PINS

Sewing pins are straight pins with either a flat or colored, round head. They are used in sewing for holding together pieces of material such as fabric or paper.

SEWING THREAD

Sewing thread is a long piece of cotton, silk, or polyester used with a needle to secure materials together. Spools of sewing thread come in a variety of colors and thicknesses.

SPOOL

A spool is a cylinder (often made of wood or plastic) on which materials like thread, wire, or tape are wound and stored.

WOODEN DOWEL

A wooden dowel is a solid, round wooden rod that comes in a variety of sizes and lengths.

tools

Adhesives, cutting tools, and paper punches are key tools used in paper-crafting projects, but tools from other craft types are also occasionally implemented. The list ahead highlights various tools plus some everyday household items that are used in the projects in this book.

adhesives

Adhesives are literally the glues for holding together components of paper-crafting projects. But adhesives can also be featured as a decorative element, as in the case of washi tape. When choosing an adhesive for your project, pay attention to the type of materials you are using, since most adhesives are designed to be used with specific materials.

The list following will help you identify the various adhesives and adhesive dispensers used in this book and in the world of paper crafting.

ADHESIVE FOAM SQUARE

An adhesive foam square is a flat foam square with adhesive on the top and bottom surfaces. It adds dimension to paper-crafted items.

CLEAR TAPE

Clear tape is a common household tape that is sticky on one side and dispensed from a roll.

CRAFT GLUE

Craft glue is a commonly used, water-based glue that is white in color and gummy in texture and dries clear.

DOUBLE-SIDED TAPE

Double-sided tape is clear tape that is sticky on both sides and dispensed from a roll.

DOUBLE-SIDED ADHESIVE TAPE GUN

One of my favorite adhesive tools, the double-sided adhesive tape gun dispenses a strip of double-sided tape. The width of the tape strip varies, and the level of adhesion can be permanent or temporary strength.

GLUE GUN

A glue gun is a tool for dispensing either cold or hot glue. Hot glue guns are particularly effective for adhering embellishments precisely and permanently to paper and other craft materials. In a hot glue gun, a glue stick is heated in the barrel, and the melted glue is dispensed from the spout.

GLUE STICK

A glue stick is a solid form of glue that comes in a push-up tube. It is a sticky adhesive that dries clear and is ideal for using on paper because it does not wrinkle the paper.

MASKING TAPE

Masking tape is an all-purpose paper tape that is easy to tear and to remove from various surfaces. The width of the tape varies as well as the strength of the adhesive.

QUICK-DRY ADHESIVE GLUE

Quick-dry adhesive glue dries quickly, making it ideal to use on projects that require a fast drying time.

SPRAY ADHESIVE

A spray adhesive works especially well for adhering thin papers to large surfaces. It will not wrinkle the paper and dries quickly.

WASHI TAPE

Washi tape is a decorative paper tape that originated in Japan. It's sticky on one side, and once placed is easy to remove to another spot. It is one of my favorite materials to use for embellishing paper crafts. It comes in an infinite selection of widths, colors, and patterns.

cutting tools

Cutting implements are essential for paper crafting, allowing you to shape materials to suit your needs. For the best results, keep your cutting tools sharp and designate certain cutting tools for use with paper and others for use with fabric, felt, or other nonpaper materials.

PAPER CUTTER

A paper cutter is a tabletop tool that can cut with precision through multiple sheets of paper at one time. A good pair of multipurpose scissors will suit most of your cutting needs, but a paper cutter (especially one with a self-sharpening blade) is a worthwhile investment for paper crafters.

ROTARY CUTTER
A rotary cutter features a sharp circular blade attached to a handle. Typically used for cutting fabric, it is also handy for cutting through medium to heavyweight paper or large sheets of paper.

SELF-HEALING CUTTING MAT
A self-healing cutting mat has a durable vinyl surface that bounces back from blade marks and cuts, enabling you to protect the tabletop or work surface beneath it. I prefer cutting mats with grid lines, which make it easy to determine measurements. A small cutting mat is ideal for smaller paper projects, while a large cutting mat is useful for fabric or large sheets of paper.

SCISSORS
It is helpful to have a few different sizes of scissors in your craft closet. A standard pair of multipurpose scissors is handy for everyday use, while a small pair with sharp tips is ideal for making fine cuts in paper or fabric. Decorative scissors—which have blades with patterned edges rather than straight edges—enable you to create interesting designs as you cut through paper, fabric, or other materials. Two popular types are scallop scissors, which create a scalloped edge, and pinking shears, which create a zigzag edge.

WIRE CUTTER
A wire cutter is an implement specifically used to cut wire, such as floral wire.

X-ACTO KNIFE
An X-ACTO knife has a very sharp, replaceable blade that is mounted to a metal, pen-like shaft. It is used for making crisp, intricate cuts in paper and other craft materials.

paper punches
Paper punches are handheld metal tools that punch shapes, like circles and hearts, out of paper. Paper punches work best on text-weight paper and lightweight cardstock.

DECORATIVE PAPER PUNCHES
Decorative paper punches create unique punched-out shapes, such as animals, flowers, letters, hearts, and circles, in various sizes, which can be used as decorative elements in a paper project.

PAPER CORNER ROUNDER
A paper corner rounder can be used to cut the pointed corner of a piece of paper into a rounded shape.

PAPER HOLE PUNCH

A paper hole punch, a common office supply tool, punches small round holes and produces confetti-like paper circles.

SCREW PUNCH

A screw punch, typically made of wood and brass, allows you to punch holes anywhere on a piece of paper (unlike standard paper hole punches, which can punch holes only along the edges of paper). A screw punch can also be used to punch holes in nonpaper materials such as fabric and leather.

miscellaneous tools

In addition to the previously listed tools, the projects in this book call for some additional tools, many of which are common household items.

BONE FOLDER

A bone folder is an essential paper-crafting tool that helps create clean, sharp folds in paper and can be used to join two pieces of paper together (see Bone Folder Techniques, page 26).

COMPUTER

A home computer is required for downloading templates that are used in the projects and for printing them out.

COOKIE CUTTERS

Cookie cutters, typically used in baking, can be used in craft projects to cut shapes from flattened clay or can be used as templates for cutting out shapes from paper and other materials.

IRON AND IRONING BOARD

An iron, typically used to remove wrinkles from fabric, can be used in craft projects to adhere iron-on elements to fabric materials. For safety and effectiveness, use the iron dry (without steam) and work on an ironing board with a heat-resistant cover.

METAL EYELET SETTER

A metal eyelet setter is a metal tool that secures a metal eyelet (page 15) to a piece of material.

PENCIL WITH ERASER

A lead pencil is handy for making erasable marks. The eraser on the end of the pencil can also be used for many purposes in paper crafting.

PENS

Pens, used for writing names and messages on your love greetings, are available in a vast variety of colors and inks, and with tips of varying sizes in many materials (such as felt-tip). A few interesting examples are gel pens, metallic pens, paint pens, and glitter pens.

PRINTER

You will need a color printer to print out the templates (see Printable Templates, page 24) that you download on your home computer and use in the projects. You will also need it to create customized cards and labels.

ROLLING PIN

A rolling pin, typically used in baking, is a cylindrical utensil that can be used to flatten clay in craft projects.

RUBBER STAMPS

Rubber stamps—made from rubber and mounted to a piece of wood or acrylic—feature carvings such as letters, numbers, or decorative shapes. Coated with ink from a stamp pad and then pressed against a surface, the stamp leaves an imprint of the carving.

RULER

In addition to being a measuring tool, a ruler can provide a stable edge when cutting paper with an X-ACTO knife. A clear ruler, which allows you to see exactly where you are cutting the paper, is an especially helpful aid for cutting straight lines with precision.

SEWING NEEDLE

A sewing needle, which has a sharp tip at one end and a small opening at the other for thread, is used for weaving the thread through material such as fabric or paper.

STAMP PADS

A stamp pad is a block saturated with ink on which you press rubber stamps so you can apply the stamp impression on a material. Stamp pads with archival ink are ideal for using in paper projects because that kind of ink will not fade over time. Stamp pads with fabric ink are appropriate for using with fabric since that ink will not smear, bleed, or fade.

TAPE MEASURE

A tape measure is a flexible ruler made from cloth, plastic, or metal. It is ideal for measuring items that have curves or corners.

WOODEN SKEWER

A wooden or bamboo skewer, typically used to thread food items together, is ideal for creating small holes in paper or other craft materials such as clay. They have a point on each end and come in a variety of diameters and lengths.

creative extras

When you're gathering your craft supplies, don't stop with just the items required in projects. Expand your creative options and customize projects to your heart's desire by also collecting embellishments, notions, and other decorative materials that catch your attention, such as glitter, sequins, stickers, confetti, and crinkle-cut paper shred. Having a well-stocked craft supply closet will invite you to think outside the box and add a truly unique touch to every love greeting you make—both those that are in this book and those that you conceive on your own.

Part of the fun of gathering supplies is exploring specialty stores and craft centers in your area and on the Internet. Your search may take you to your local art supply and craft stores, the hardware store, floral supply stores, fabric and yarn stores, grocery stores, and even restaurant and baking supply stores. Also check out local vintage shops or flea markets for vintage papers or embellishments that can add a special touch to your love greeting. And since many of the projects include edible treats, check out your local candy store or food import store for tasty and visually appealing candies and other goodies. You can also visit the local farmers' market to see what sweets artisans in your area are making. When I travel to a new country or city, I am always on the lookout for fun new goodies to bring home and add to my stash. You can also source creative materials from the comfort of your own home via Etsy, eBay, and other online websites. There are many online stores that offer fun and interesting materials perfect for creating love greetings. (I've included my favorite sources in the Resources section at the back of the book.) There are treasures to be found everywhere!

tips & techniques

The following tips and techniques offer basic guidance on using some of the tools, materials, and processes that are called for in this book's projects. Review them before getting started, and you'll have an easier and more enjoyable time creating your love greetings.

tips

You might already be familiar with these basic paper-crafting tools, but these tips may help you avoid common usage pitfalls.

printable templates

• "Printables" are designs that you download on your computer from www.chroniclebooks .com/bemine, print out, cut out, and incorporate into the project as instructed. More than a dozen projects in this book call for a printable. Using the printables will enable you to make the project exactly as I have designed it, so the final product will look very similar to what you see in the photograph that accompanies each project. Print out a printable, either on your home printer or by taking the PDF to a local copy shop and using their printing services. Create a "Be Mine printables" folder on your computer's desktop, where you can store all the project printables you've downloaded. That way, you can easily access them at any time.

paper punches

• If you want to punch a hole from a particular spot on a piece of paper, make light pencil marks to help you align the punching tool with the area to be punched.

• After repeated use, paper punches can sometimes "stick." Punching the tool through waxed paper several times will loosen up the punch.

• If you find that your punching tool is not creating crisp paper shapes, sharpen it by punching it through aluminum foil several times.

• Store paper punches in plastic bins with lids to avoid exposure to moisture, which can rust metal paper punches.

rubber stamps

• After imprinting a piece of paper with a stamp, leave adequate time for the ink to dry before handling the paper.

• To produce a crisp stamping, apply the ink to the stamp by holding the carving-side up and placing the inkpad on top of the rubber stamp. This technique will ensure that you apply an even layer of ink.

• Before using the stamp in your project, test out the stamp and stamp pad first to ensure that you have an adequate amount of ink on the stamp and that you are applying enough pressure to make an even impression.

• Clean your rubber stamps after you use them and before you store them by applying a rubber stamp cleaner with a damp washcloth. Do not use cleaning agents such as baby wipes, because the alcohol in the wipes will dry out the rubber, leading to cracking. Do not place wood-mounted stamps under running water, since this will damage the wood and loosen the stamp from the wooden mount.

• Store rubber stamps upright, away from direct sunlight, at room temperature.

x-acto knife

Safety is of utmost importance when using an X-ACTO knife. Here are some tips to help you avoid injury:

• Make sure the metal collar holding the blade in place is tightly secured.

• Keep your fingers away from the blade, and when cutting through a material, apply firm and even pressure at a 45-degree angle to the work surface.

• Always use with a self-healing cutting mat under the material to avoid damaging your work surface.

• Change blades regularly to avoid injuries caused by dull blades.

techniques

Here are a few simple techniques you will want to learn before taking on some of the projects in this book. You will also be able to apply these techniques to future craft projects.

sewing techniques

A few projects in this book call for sewing skills and tools. A sewing machine will get the job done faster, but a needle and thread will enable you to complete the project just as well. Whether you are using a sewing machine or a needle and thread, there's only one stitch you need to know: the running stitch, also called the straight stitch.

RUNNING STITCH

In this basic sewing stitch, a threaded needle is passed in and out of a piece of material, such as paper or fabric. The stitch length can vary, and the resulting stitch looks like a straight dashed line. When using a sewing machine select the straight stitch setting on your sewing machine and use the machine as directed. If stitching by hand, begin by passing a threaded needle up through the back side of the paper or fabric. Then poke the needle back down through the front side of the material, close to where you initially came through, and pull the thread down and completely through to the back side. Repeat, being mindful to create a straight line with your stitches and leave an even amount of space between stitches. When you're finished, pass the needle through to the back side of the work, cut the thread leaving a tail a few inches long, tie a secure knot close to the material, and clip the ends of the thread with a pair of small, sharp sewing scissors.

bone folder techniques

A bone folder ensures neat, crisp folds in paper. It's especially important to use a bone folder when working with cardstock or heavy-weight paper that can crack when folded. Folding is not all you will do with a bone folder. Scoring and burnishing are additional techniques you'll find handy for completing some of the projects in this book. Note: When using a bone folder, use a self-healing cutting mat under the material you are folding to protect your work surface.

SCORING

Scoring is the first step to a neat fold. Scoring creates a slightly depressed line on the surface you are about to fold. To score, place the edge of a ruler where you want to make a fold. Place the tip of the bone folder against the ruler's edge and slide the bone folder alongside the ruler, bearing down into the paper, until you have scored the desired line into the paper.

FOLDING

After you have scored the paper, fold the paper over the scored line (so the scored line is hidden in the fold). Then press the side of the bone folder firmly against the crease of the folded paper and slide it along the folded edge to neatly flatten it.

BURNISHING

Another function of a bone folder is to burnish paper, or to adhere two pieces of paper together. Once adhesive or glue has been applied between the papers, run the long side of the bone folder over the surface of the paper, which will neatly distribute the adhesive and create a strong bond.

projects

i'm sweet on you matchbox

Everyone loves to receive a little box of sweet treats. This cute, colorful matchbox is perfect for holding a handful of candies that will brighten up anyone's day. You can also fill the box with fun trinkets, photographs, or love notes instead.

MATERIALS

I'm Sweet On You Matchbox printable, three pages: Patterned Paper, Box Pieces, and Labels

2 sheets of white cardstock, 8½ by 11 in/21.5 by 28 cm

TOOLS

Computer and printer

X-ACTO knife

Ruler

Self-healing cutting mat

Bone folder

Glue stick

HOW TO

1 With your computer, download this project's printable from www.chroniclebooks.com/bemine.

2 Print the Patterned Paper printable onto one sheet of white cardstock.

3 Put the white cardstock back into the printer so its blank side can be printed on. Then print the Box Pieces printable on the blank side.

→

4 Using the X-ACTO knife, ruler, and self-healing cutting mat, cut out the box pieces (inner box and outer box) along the solid lines. (On the inner box piece, be sure to cut along the short solid line that appears in each corner.)

5 Using the ruler and bone folder, score both box pieces along the dashed lines.

6 To form the inner compartment of the box, fold the inner box piece along the scored lines. Using the glue stick, place glue on the corner flaps. Then tuck them against the inner side of the box and press with your fingers to secure them in place. To form the outer case of the box, fold the outer box piece along the scored lines and apply glue to the underside of the folding edge that is slightly wider than the other folding edge. Press the glued flap against the opposite outer flap, creating the outer case of the box. Let dry for 15 minutes and then slide the inner compartment into the outer case.

7 Print the Labels printable onto the remaining white cardstock. Using the X-ACTO knife, ruler, and self-healing cutting mat, cut out one message label.

8 Using the glue stick, apply glue to the back side of the message label and wrap it around the top of the box, smoothing to adhere it.

VARIATIONS
- Substitute the "I'm Sweet on You" message with your own message by writing it on a strip of paper and then adhering it to the box.
- Instead of affixing a message to the box, tie a brightly colored ribbon around it.

fingerprint heart wrapping paper

Literally leave your mark by creating hearts with your own stamped fingerprints. This is a fun project for kids to work on because it is easy and personal (and of course a little messy!). Make this wrapping paper as the finishing touch on a gift for a special friend or relative. Or try making gift tags or cards using the fingerprint heart technique.

MATERIALS

1 sq yd/91 sq cm of white kraft paper

TOOLS

Masking tape
Stamp pad with archival ink

HOW TO

1 Place the piece of white kraft paper face up on the work surface. To stabilize it, place a small piece of masking tape on each of the four corners.

→

2 Place the fingertip of your pointer finger on the stamp pad, rolling it back and forth to ensure the ink is evenly distributed across the fingertip. Place the fingertip onto the kraft paper at a slight diagonal to the left, and press the fingertip to the paper. The resulting mark will make one half of a heart print. To make the other half of the heart print, re-ink the fingertip and press it at a slight diagonal in the opposite direction (to the right), overlapping the bottom of the first fingerprint. Continue making heart prints on the kraft paper, spaced apart at whatever distance you prefer.

3 Let the ink dry for 1 hour, then remove the masking tape from the corners of the kraft paper. Your wrapping paper is ready to use.

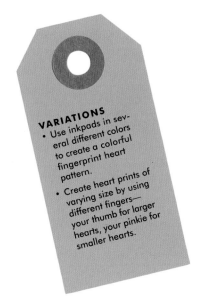

VARIATIONS
- Use inkpads in several different colors to create a colorful fingerprint heart pattern.
- Create heart prints of varying size by using different fingers—your thumb for larger hearts, your pinkie for smaller hearts.

message in a bottle

We might not all have the chance to discover a message in a bottle washed up on the seashore, but we *can* create our own to give to someone special. The bottle is a creative and memorable way to send a love greeting, and the recipient will love unwrapping the secret message inside. You can find small glass bottles with cork stoppers at your local craft or hobby store.

MATERIALS

Message in a Bottle printable, one page

1 piece of white text-weight paper, 5½ by 8½ in/14 by 21.5 cm

1 piece of blue scrap paper, 3 by 3 in/7.5 by 7.5 cm

1 piece of yellow scrap paper, 3 by 3 in/7.5 by 7.5 cm

1 piece of twine, 7 in/17.5 cm

Glass bottle with cork top

TOOLS

Computer and printer

Self-healing cutting mat

X-ACTO knife

Ruler

Glue stick

Heart paper punch, with ³⁄₈-in/1-cm heart hole

Scissors

→

I LOVE YOU TO THE MOON AND BACK.

1 With your computer, download this project's printable from www.chroniclebooks.com/bemine.

2 Print the Message in a Bottle printable onto the white text-weight paper.

3 Place the printed page on the self-healing cutting mat and, using the X-ACTO knife and ruler, cut out the two components (the "I Love You to the Moon and Back" message and the patterned paper rectangle), cutting neatly along the edges of each.

4 Apply the glue stick to the underside of the patterned paper. Place the patterned paper piece glue-side down on the underside of the message paper piece. Press the two pieces against the work surface and smooth your fingers across the surface of the message, to stick them to each other. Let the glue dry for 15 minutes.

5 Using the heart paper punch, create heart confetti by punching holes in the blue and yellow scrap paper.

6 Roll up the message so the patterned paper faces out and the message faces in. Wrap the twine around the rolled up message and tie a bow to secure it. Use the scissors to trim the ends of the twine so they are even in length.

7 Place the rolled up message and heart confetti into the glass bottle. Secure the cork lid on top of the glass bottle.

VARIATIONS
- Place a few small candies in the glass bottle for an extra sweet treat.
- Instead of using the printable, write your own custom message on a strip of paper.

peek-a-boo heart card

Say "peek-a-boo!" The photograph hidden under the heart on this card is a fun surprise for the recipient. Photo booth strip pictures are the perfect size, but you can use any small photo that will send a heartfelt message.

MATERIALS

1 piece of colored cardstock, 2½ by 4¼ in/6 by 10.5 cm

1 photograph, 2 by 2 in/5 by 5 cm

1 piece of gray cardstock, 4¼ by 5½ in/10.5 by 14 cm

TOOLS

Pencil with eraser

Ruler

Self-healing cutting mat

X-ACTO knife

Bone folder

Glue stick

HOW TO

1 Using the pencil and ruler, draw a heart that is 2 by 1¾ in/5 by 4.5 cm in the center of the colored cardstock.

2 Place the colored cardstock on the self-healing cutting mat and, using the X-ACTO knife, cut around the edge of the entire left half of the heart. Erase any visible pencil marks.

→

3 Using the ruler and bone folder, score down the center of the heart. Lift the left half of the heart and bend it toward the right along the scored line, making a vertical fold down the center of the heart.

4 Position the photograph on the underside of the colored cardstock, so that when the left half of the heart is lifted, the photograph is revealed. Once you have placed the photo where you want it, apply glue to the outer edges of its front surface. Then press the photo to the underside of the cardstock to secure it in place.

5 Using the glue stick, apply glue to the underside of the colored cardstock and position it across the center of the piece of gray cardstock. Let dry for 15 minutes.

VARIATIONS
- Instead of revealing a photograph, reveal a personalized written message.
- Use patterned paper instead of colored cardstock.

hearts in a tube

Surprise! As your loved one opens the lid of this greeting, a "Happy Valentine's Day!" message will be revealed. Add confetti or sweet treats to the mailing tube for an extra special surprise.

MATERIALS

Hearts in a Tube printable, two pages: Patterned Paper and Heart Letters

2 sheets of white sticker paper, 8½ by 11 in/21.5 by 28 cm

1 cardboard mailing tube with a cap on each end, maximum 2¼ in/5.5 cm in diameter and 9½ in/24 cm long

1 sheet of colored cardstock, 8½ by 11 in/21.5 by 28 cm

1 piece of twine, 50 in/127 cm long

20 pieces of washi tape, 1 in/2.5 cm long

TOOLS

Computer and printer

Tape measure

Piece of scrap paper

Pencil

Ruler

Scissors

Circle paper punch, 1½ in/4 cm in diameter

Circle paper punch, 1 in/2.5 cm in diameter

Pen

→

1 With your computer, download this project's printable from www.chroniclebooks.com/bemine.

2 Print out the two pages, Patterned Paper and Heart Letters, onto the front side of the two sheets of white sticker paper.

3 Using the tape measure, measure the length and diameter of the cardboard mailing tube. Write down the measurements on the piece of scrap paper, adding 1 in/2.5 cm to the width.

4 Using the pencil and ruler, mark the measurements on the back side of the patterned paper and draw lines connecting them, creating a rectangle. Using the scissors, cut out the patterned paper rectangle along the lines.

5 Remove the sticker backing from the patterned paper. Wrap the patterned paper rectangle around the mailing tube, gently pressing down the outer edges to adhere to the cardboard tube. Make sure a cap is placed on the bottom end of the cardboard tube.

6 Using the 1½-in/4-cm circle paper punch, punch out 20 circles from the colored cardstock.

7 Using the 1-in/2.5-cm circle paper punch, punch out all the circles on the heart letters sticker paper sheet.

8 Peel off the backing from one of the sticker heart letters and place it on the center of a colored cardstock circle. Repeat with the remaining letters and then put the letter pieces in order on your work surface to create the greeting "Happy Valentine's Day!"

9 Place the first letter piece of the greeting ("H") face down on the work surface. Then measure 8 in/20 cm from one end of the length of twine; this is where you will attach the first letter piece. Place the 8-in/20-cm point on the twine over the center of the back side of the paper circle and place one of the pieces of washi tape over the twine to secure it in place. Leaving a gap of ¼ in/ 6 mm between each letter, continue placing the letters in order, using a piece of washi tape to secure the twine to each letter.

10 After you have attached all the letters to the twine—creating a message garland—secure the beginning end of the twine (the "H" end) to the underside of the top cap (the lid) of the mailing tube with a piece of washi tape. Put the rest of the garland inside the mailing tube.

11 Use a pen to write "Open Here" on the top cap of the mailing tube. Insert the cap to secure the contents.

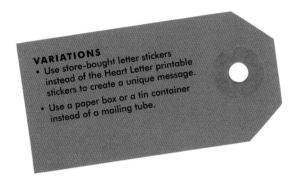

VARIATIONS
- Use store-bought letter stickers instead of the Heart Letter printable stickers to create a unique message.
- Use a paper box or a tin container instead of a mailing tube.

YOU MAKE ME SMILE

stitched confetti valentine

I love giving a valentine that is also a little gift. Filling a vellum heart with confetti and adding a special message makes this project festive and fun. The translucence of the vellum allows your recipient to see the goodies inside. Feel free to add other little mementos in the valentine, such as photographs or ticket stubs, before stitching it up.

MATERIALS

5 pieces of colored vellum, 6 by 6 in/15 by 15 cm, in five different colors

1 piece of white text-weight paper, 6 by 6 in/15 by 15 cm

2 pieces of clear vellum, 6 by 6 in/15 by 15 cm

1 strip of white text-weight paper, ½ by 2 in/1.2 cm by 5 cm

1 piece of colored thread, 20 in/50 cm long, if using a sewing needle (or on a spool, if using a sewing machine)

TOOLS

Hole punch, with ¼-in/6-mm hole

Paper punch, with ½-in/12-mm-diameter circular hole

Scissors

Pencil

Pen

Sewing needle (or sewing machine)

HOW TO

1 Using the hole punch and the paper punch, create confetti by punching holes through the sheets of colored vellum paper.

→

2 Fold the white text-weight paper in half. Using the scissors, cut out a one-half heart shape that, when opened, is approximately 5 in/12 cm wide and 5 in/12 cm tall.

3 Place the paper heart onto one piece of clear vellum. Using the pencil, trace around the paper heart. Repeat this step with the second piece of vellum. Using the scissors, cut out the hearts from both pieces of vellum.

4 With the pen, write out a love-themed message on the strip of white text-weight paper.

5 Thread the sewing needle (or sewing machine) with the colored thread.

6 Place the two clear vellum hearts on top of each other so the edges are aligned. While holding the two vellum hearts together, and using the threaded sewing needle (or sewing machine), sew a running stitch around the heart, 1/8 in/3 mm from the edge. Start sewing near the bottom of the heart, leaving a 2½-in/6-cm opening at the top.

7 Insert the confetti into the opening of the heart and then insert the message strip, placing it in the middle of the heart on top of the confetti. Stitch the opening closed.

VARIATIONS
- In addition to or in place of confetti, add small candies or mementos inside of the heart.
- To create a hanging valentine, punch a hole at the top of the heart and thread ribbon through the hole.

you blow me away
paper pinwheel

This versatile project can be enjoyed in many ways: Personalize the message and give it to a friend; use it as a decorative gift topper; or place it in a glass vase filled with candies for a cute table centerpiece. Patterned paper straws come in a variety of colors and patterns and can be found at craft stores and specialty food stores.

MATERIALS

You Blow Me Away Paper Pinwheel printable, two pages: Patterned Paper and Message Labels

1 sheet of white text-weight paper, 8½ by 11 in/21.5 by 28 cm

1 piece of white sticker paper, 5½ by 8½ in/14 by 21.5 cm

1 sheet of colored text-weight paper, 8½ by 11 in/21.5 by 28 cm

Sewing pin with a ⅛-in/3-mm colored round head

Bead with a hole ¹⁄₁₆ in/2 mm in diameter

Paper straw

Eraser from end of a pencil

TOOLS

Computer and printer

X-ACTO knife

Ruler

Self-healing cutting mat

Pencil

Glue stick

Wire cutter

YOU BLOW ME AWAY!

1 With your computer, download this project's printable from www.chroniclebooks.com/bemine.

2 Print the Patterned Paper printable onto the white text-weight paper.

3 Print the Message Labels printable onto the front of the white sticker paper.

4 Using the X-ACTO knife, ruler, and self-healing cutting mat, neatly cut out one label along its outer edge.

5 Using the pencil, ruler, and self-healing cutting mat, draw a 5-in/12-cm square on the patterned paper. With the X-ACTO knife and ruler, cut out the patterned paper square. Lay the patterned paper square on the colored text-weight paper, and with the X-ACTO knife and ruler, cut out an identically sized square on the colored text-weight paper.

6 Using the glue stick, apply glue to the underside of the patterned paper square and press it against the surface of the solid colored square to join the pieces together. Allow 15 minutes to dry.

7 Fold the paper square diagonally in half, and then unfold the square. Then fold the square across the opposite diagonal, and unfold the square. An X will now appear across the surface of the paper square, marking the folds.

8 Using the X-ACTO knife, ruler, and self-healing cutting mat, cut along each of the folds, starting from the outer corner of the square and stopping three-fourths

→

of the way to the center of the square. Without making a crease in the paper, draw in every other point so the four points overlap at the center of the square.

9 Place the sewing pin through the corner points and through the center of the front of the square. Then flip the paper square over so you're looking at the back side. Thread the bead onto the pin, and then insert the sharp tip of the sewing pin through the paper straw ½ in/12 mm from the top of the straw. Using the wire cutters, trim the end of the pin so ½ in/ 12 mm of the pin remains. Insert the remaining length of the pin into the pencil eraser so the point is safely embedded in the eraser.

10 To apply the label to the straw, remove the sticker backing from the label and then place it around the straw so the two ends are the same length. Press the two ends together to secure the label in place.

VARIATIONS
- Instead of using the Patterned Paper printable, use patterned and solid-color origami paper to create the pinwheel.
- For added flair, glue a mini pom-pom or a button to the center of the pinwheel.

paper heart box

We all have fond memories of the quintessential Valentine's Day gift, a red heart box of chocolates. For a modern twist on that tradition, make a Paper Heart Box and personalize it with a name or clever message. The heart box can be filled with candies, trinkets, photographs, or love notes.

MATERIALS

Paper Heart Box printable, two pages: Hearts and Box Side Pieces

2 sheets of red cardstock, 8½ by 11 in/21.5 by 28 cm

White letter stickers, ½ in/12 mm tall, for message of your choice

TOOLS

Computer and printer

Scissors

X-ACTO knife

Ruler

Self-healing cutting mat

Quick-dry adhesive glue

HOW TO

1 With your computer, download this project's printable from www.chroniclebooks.com/bemine.

2 Print both printable pages (Hearts and Box Side Pieces) onto the red cardstock.

3 Using the scissors, cut out the two heart shapes (Top Heart and Bottom Heart) from the Hearts printable.

→

4 Using the X-ACTO knife, ruler, and self-healing cutting mat, and cutting along the solid lines, cut out all four Box Side Pieces (two labeled "bottom point" and two labeled "top point").

5 Fold the four box side pieces along all the dashed lines.

6 Attach one of the box side pieces labeled "bottom point" to the bottom half of the top heart in this way: Lay the top heart on the work surface. Arrange the box side piece in a V-shape, and position it so the folded tabs are around the edge of the bottom surface of the top heart and are folded in toward each other, and its V-shape aligns with the V-shape of the bottom heart.

7 Apply glue to the underside of each tab and then attach each tab to the underside of the top heart $1/16$ in/2 mm in from the edge. Hold the tabs in place for several minutes until the glue dries.

8 Attach one of the box side pieces labeled "top point" to the top half of the top heart, following the instructions in step 7.

9 You'll find that the ends of the two side pieces will overlap. Apply glue to the overlapping ends and secure them together.

10 Repeat steps 6 through 9, using the bottom heart piece and the two remaining box side pieces. But this time, glue the tabs of the box side pieces $1/8$ in/3 mm in from the edge of the heart. This will allow the top and bottom of the box to close neatly.

11 Using the white letter stickers, create a message on the surface of the top heart.

VARIATIONS
- Fill the box with crinkle cut paper shred or confetti.
- Place mini cupcake liners inside the box and fill each liner with a treat or trinket.
- Create Paper Heart Boxes in different sizes by adjusting the size settings on your printer.

conversation heart card

Pass along a special message with these clay hearts reminiscent of traditional conversation heart candies. The malleable nature of polymer clay makes it easy to roll out, cut with cookie cutters, take clear stamped impressions, and harden when baked in an oven. Make the hearts in a bunch of sizes and use various stamps to imprint personalized messages. Affix to a card or use as a gift tag. The messages are just as sweet as candy and last much longer!

MATERIALS

Small ball of colored polymer clay, about 1 in/2.5 cm in diameter

1 piece of cardstock, 4¼ by 5½ in/10.5 by 14 cm

1 piece of twine, 5 in/12 cm long

TOOLS

1 piece of parchment paper, 8 by 12 in/20 by 30.5 cm

Rolling pin

Ruler

1 heart-shaped cookie cutter, 1½ in/4 cm wide

Alphabet letter stamps, with letters no taller than ¼ in/6 mm

Wooden skewer, ⅛ in/3 mm in diameter

Baking sheet

Oven

Self-healing cutting mat

Pencil

Screw punch, with ⅛-in-/3-mm-diameter bit

Scissors

→

1 Place the piece of parchment paper on the flat work surface. Soften the ball of clay by kneading it with your hands and then place it on the parchment paper. Using the rolling pin and the ruler, roll out the clay to a $1/8$-in/3-mm thickness.

2 Using the heart-shaped cookie cutter, cut out a heart from the clay.

3 Create a message on the clay heart by gently pressing the alphabet letter stamps into the clay. (I recommend practicing your stamping technique on a sample clay heart first, so you know how hard to press on the stamp to obtain a clear impression in the clay.)

4 Create a hole in the top right area of the clay heart by poking the wooden skewer through it.

5 Lift the parchment paper and place it on a baking sheet. Bake the clay heart in the oven according to the clay manufacturer's instructions.

6 Place the cardstock vertically on the self-healing cutting mat. Use the pencil and the ruler to make two marks in the center of the card, one that is 2 in/5 cm down from the top center edge of the card and another that is $2 1/4$ in/5.5 cm down from the top center edge of the card. Using the screw punch, punch holes through the pencil marks.

7 After the clay heart has finished baking and has completely cooled, string the twine through the hole in the heart, entering through the top and then threading through the bottom hole in the card. Then thread the other end of the twine through the top hole in the card, so both ends are on the underside of the card. Secure the twine ends with a knot and trim the ends with scissors.

VARIATIONS
- Instead of using alphabet letter stamps to create a message, use a felt-tip pen with permanent ink to write a message on the fully baked clay heart.
- To make a glitter heart, brush a layer of clear glue on the baked clay heart and generously sprinkle glitter on it. Let the glue dry for 5 hours and then shake off the excess glitter.

heart lollipop cover

A lollipop can brighten anyone's day! Replace a plain lollipop wrapper with a customized cover for a gift that's sure to make your loved one smile. Heart Lollipop Covers transform lollipops into special gifts or party favors. For an added personal touch, write a special message on the cover to each recipient.

MATERIALS

Heart Lollipop Cover printable, two pages: Lollipop Covers and Lollipop Cover Labels

1 sheet of colored cardstock, 8½ by 11 in/21.5 by 28 cm

1 sheet of white sticker paper, 5½ by 8½ in/14 by 21.5 cm

1 flat lollipop with a maximum diameter of 1¼ in/3 cm

TOOLS

Computer and printer

Self-healing cutting mat

X-ACTO knife

Ruler

Bone folder

Hole punch, with ⅛-in/3-mm hole

Glue stick

HOW TO

1 With your computer, download this project's printable from www.chroniclebooks.com/bemine.

→

2 Print out the Lollipop Covers printable onto the colored cardstock.

3 Print out the Lollipop Cover Labels printable onto the white sticker paper.

4 Lay the lollipop covers on the self-healing cutting mat. Using the X-ACTO knife and ruler, cut out one of the lollipop covers along the solid lines.

5 Using the bone folder, ruler, and self-healing cutting mat, score along the dashed lines of the lollipop cover. Fold the cardstock along the scored lines and smooth down the folds with the bone folder.

6 Using the hole punch, punch a hole at the center of the lollipop cover flap where there is a small circle.

7 Using the X-ACTO knife, ruler, and self-healing cutting mat, cut out one of the lollipop cover labels by cutting along the solid line.

8 Remove the sticker backing and center the lollipop cover label across the front of the lollipop cover. Press down the label and wrap it around the cover, smoothing to adhere it.

9 Slide the stick of the lollipop down through the lollipop cover, so the lollipop is nestled inside the cover. Using the glue stick, apply glue to the outside surface of the cover end flap on the back side of the cover. Tuck under the end flap and press to adhere.

VARIATIONS
- Cut out a photograph and adhere it to the front of the lollipop cover.
- Instead of using the Lollipop Cover Labels printable, adhere a strip of patterned scrapbook paper to the surface of the lollipop cover.

felt heart pouch

Place candies or tiny trinkets inside this Felt Heart Pouch for a sweetly packaged love greeting. Wool felt is a wonderful material to work with because it doesn't fray when cut, and it comes in a wide variety of colors, blends, and weights. Tip: Make a larger version of the Felt Heart Pouch by printing out the shapes at a larger size.

MATERIALS

Felt Heart Pouch printable, one page

1 sheet of white text-weight paper, 8½ by 11 in/21.5 by 28 cm

1 piece of white twill tape, 4 in/10 cm long and ½ in/12 mm wide

1 piece of wool felt in any color, 5 by 9 in/12 by 23 cm

1 piece of cotton embroidery thread, in any color, 21 in/53 cm long

TOOLS

Computer and printer

Alphabet letter rubber stamps, with letters no taller than ½ in/12 mm

Stamp pad with fabric ink in any color

Scissors

Pen

Sewing needle

Straight pins

→

1 With your computer, download this project's printable from www.chroniclebooks.com/bemine.

2 Print the Felt Heart Pouch printable onto the piece of white text-weight paper.

3 Fold the twill tape in half. Using the alphabet letter stamps and stamp pad, stamp the letters onto the center of the folded twill tape, spelling out the name of the recipient. Let dry for 1 hour.

4 Using the scissors, cut out the three shapes on the printable along the solid lines. Place the three paper shapes on the wool felt piece. Using the pen, trace the outline of each of the three shapes on the felt. Using the scissors, cut out the three shapes from the felt.

5 Thread the embroidery thread on the sewing needle, double it up, and tie a knot at the end. Bring the needle up through the felt, from back to front, at one corner of the bottom edge of the felt "Top Heart" shape (the thread knot will be at the back of your work). Sew a running stitch along the bottom edge to the opposite corner.

6 Place the felt "Bottom Heart" shape on top of the felt "Back Heart" shape, making sure the edges are matched up. Then place the felt "Top Heart" shape— with the needle and thread still in place—on top of the other two shapes, making sure the edges line up. (The three shapes should now make the shape of a single heart.) Using the straight pins, pin the three pieces together.

→

7 Pin the personalized twill tape tag to the upper right-hand side of the heart, making sure the ends of the tag are tucked between the heart shapes.

8 Using the threaded needle, continue sewing a running stitch around the edge of the heart, sewing the heart shapes together. Knot the thread on the back side of the heart and, using the scissors, cut the thread.

VARIATIONS
- To create a unique color-block heart, use a different color of felt for each of the three heart shapes.
- For a special personalized touch, place tiny photographs or handwritten messages in the Felt Heart Pouch.

tic-tac-toe card

Combine sweet treats with a game, and you have the perfect little love greeting. Little kids and big kids alike will adore the card (and candy). If you want to give a sugar-free card, try replacing the candy with figurines or stickers in two different colors or designs.

MATERIALS

Tic-Tac-Toe Card printable, three pages: Tic-Tac-Toe Card, From Labels, and Xs & Os Labels

1 sheet of white cardstock, 5½ by 8½ in/14 by 21.5 cm

2 sheets of white sticker paper, 8½ by 11 in/21.5 by 28 cm

1 clear self-sealing envelope, 2½ by 2½ in/6 by 6 cm

16 small candies, 8 in one color and 8 in another color

1 clear self-sealing envelope, 5⅝ by 8¾ in/14 by 22 cm

TOOLS

Computer and printer
X-ACTO knife
Ruler
Self-healing cutting mat
Pen

HOW TO

1 With your computer, download this project's printable from www.chroniclebooks.com/bemine.

→

TIC-TAC-TOE

TIC-TAC-TOE
Xs & Os

YOUR FRIEND, *Judah*

2 Print out the Tic-Tac-Toe Card printable onto the white cardstock.

3 Print out both pages of labels (the From Labels and the Xs & Os Labels) onto the front of the two sheets of white sticker paper.

4 Using the X-ACTO knife, ruler, and self-healing cutting mat, cut out one from label and one Xs and Os label, cutting along the solid lines.

5 Using the pen, sign your name on the from label (underneath "From Your Friend") and on the tic-tac-toe card (next to "Your Friend").

6 Remove the sticker backing from the Xs & Os label and adhere the label to the small envelope, wrapping it across the envelope from back to front so "Xs & Os" appears centered on the front. Fill the envelope with the sixteen candies and seal the envelope. (Candies can be used as tic-tac-toe playing pieces.)

7 Remove the sticker backing from the from label and adhere the label to the large envelope, wrapping it across the envelope from back to front so the words "Happy Valentine's Day" appear centered on the front.

8 Place the tic-tac-toe card and the Xs & Os envelope inside the large clear envelope and seal the envelope.

VARIATIONS
- Laminate the tic-tac-toe card so it can be used for years to come.
- Instead of using candies, put X and O letter stickers on circular wooden disks to create reusable playing pieces.

personalized felt heart card

Everyone appreciates something made especially for them. Create a unique handmade card by personalizing a felt heart with iron-on letters. Felt comes in a variety of colors and weights, and iron-on letters come in various fonts and colors, so you can mix and match to customize your hearts for each recipient.

MATERIALS

1 square of wool felt, 3 by 3 in/7.5 by 7.5 cm

White soft-flocked iron-on letters, 1 in/2.5 cm

1 piece of colored cardstock, 4¼ by 5½ in/10.5 by 14 cm

TOOLS

Scissors

Ironing board

Iron

Glue stick

HOW TO

1 Using the scissors, cut out a heart shape, approximately 2½ in/6 cm wide and 2 in/5 cm tall, from the wool felt.

2 Using an ironing board as your work surface, cut out one iron-on letter and place it, adhesive-side down, in the center of the felt heart. Preheat the iron (dry, no steam) on the medium-high setting. Press the letter down on the felt for 15 seconds, then flip over the felt piece and press for 10 seconds on the back side. →

3 Let the iron-on letter cool for 2 minutes. Peel off the backing from the iron-on letter.

4 With the glue stick, apply glue to the back side of the felt heart, and center it on the front of the cardstock. With your hand, press down on the felt heart to affix it to the card.

5 Let dry for 30 minutes.

VARIATIONS
- Personalize other items, such as muslin bags and gift bags, by attaching a personalized felt heart.
- Substitute felt with fabric and create a personalized fabric heart card.

message on a spool

This love greeting is a distinctive way to show what a fool (or spool) for love you are. You can print or hand-letter the message to your loved one. Increase the paper length, and you can write a message as long as you want—even a letter! To create a more colorful Message on a Spool, use colored paper, a colored spool, and colorful twine.

MATERIALS

Message on a Spool printable, one page

1 sheet of white text-weight paper, 8½ by 11 in/21.5 by 28 cm

1 metal eyelet, ⅛ in/3 mm

Cotton twine

Washi tape

Spool, no larger than 2 in/5 cm tall

TOOLS

Computer and printer

X-ACTO knife

Ruler

Self-healing cutting mat

Paper hole punch, with ⅛-in/3-mm hole

Metal eyelet setter

Scissors

→

I AM A SPOOL IN LOVE WITH YOU!

HOW TO

1 With your computer, download this project's printable from www.chroniclebooks.com/bemine.

2 Print the Message on a Spool printable onto the white text-weight paper.

3 Using the X-ACTO knife, ruler, and self-healing cutting mat, cut out one of the "I am a Spool in Love with You" message strips from the printable.

4 Using the paper hole punch, punch a hole at the left edge of the message where there is a small circle. Using the metal eyelet setter, set the metal eyelet through the punched hole, following the manufacturer's instructions.

5 Using the scissors and ruler, cut a 12-in/30.5-cm piece of cotton twine. Insert the twine through the eyelet and pull the twine through until the two ends are the same length. Tie the ends into a knot that rests at the edge of the paper strip.

6 With a piece of washi tape, secure the right edge of the paper strip to the wooden spool. Wind the paper strip around the spool until snug. Wrap the two ends of the twine around the wooden spool in opposite directions and tie them in a bow.

VARIATIONS
- Instead of using the Message on a Spool printable, write your own message on a strip of paper roughly 3/4 in/2 cm wide.
- If using a spool made of unfinished wood, paint the spool a bright color before beginning the project.

vellum heart card

Vellum is a versatile translucent paper that comes in a variety of colors. Overlapping pieces of vellum paper can create a stunning stained-glass window effect. To make a special handmade card, use vellum circles to compose a heart shape. You can also place the vellum circles on the card to make a letter of the alphabet or some other shape.

MATERIALS

4 pieces of vellum paper of different colors, 4 by 4 in/10 by 10 cm

1 piece of white cardstock, 4¼ by 5½ in/10.5 by 14 cm

TOOLS

Hole punch, with ¼-in/6-mm hole

Glue stick

HOW TO

1 Using the hole punch, punch out circles from the colored vellum paper.

2 Place glue on one side of each of the vellum circles and adhere them to the white cardstock, so that they overlap and, all together, form a heart shape.

VARIATIONS
- Use text-weight paper or cardstock instead of vellum paper.
- Use a decorative paper punch, such as a heart-shaped punch, instead of a hole punch.

bunny balloon card

The perfect sugar-free valentine! This adorable card comes with a little gift, a heart balloon, which the recipient can either blow up or keep intact on the card. You can find heart-shaped balloons in a variety of colors at your local party supply store or on the Internet.

MATERIALS

Balloon Bunny Card printable, two pages: a "Happy Valentine's Day!" card and an "I Love You!" card

1 piece of white cardstock, 4¼ by 5½ in/10.5 by 14 cm

Heart-shaped balloon

TOOLS

Computer and printer

Screw punch, with ⅛-in/3-mm bit

1 piece of washi tape, 1 in/2.5 cm long

HOW TO

1 With your computer, download this project's printable from www.chroniclebooks.com/bemine.

2 Choose which card you want to create—either the "Happy Valentine's Day!" card or the "I Love You!" card. Print the chosen printable onto the front of the white cardstock.

3 Using the screw punch, punch a hole in the card at the top end of the printed string line where there is a small circle.

→

4 Thread the balloon through the hole, from the back of the card to the front, until the whole balloon except for the rolled end has been pulled through to the front of the card.

5 Secure the rolled end of the balloon to the back side of the card with the piece of washi tape.

VARIATIONS

• For added dimension, inflate the balloon after you have pulled most of it through the hole, then tie a knot in the balloon end and proceed to step 5.

• Instead of using a heart-shaped balloon, use a round balloon and write a love-themed message on it with a permanent felt-tip pen.

accordion envelope card

Give the gift of taking a trip down memory lane with this Accordion Envelope Card. Perfect for many different occasions, the envelopes can be filled with special mementos, photographs, notes, and trinkets for your loved one. Envelopes come in a variety of colors and textures, so you can create a monochromatic look or mix and match envelope colors and surfaces.

MATERIALS

5 paper envelopes, 3⅝ by 5⅛ in/9 by 12.5 cm

1 colored metal brad

1 piece of cotton ribbon, 16 in/40.5 cm long and ¼ in/6 mm wide

TOOLS

X-ACTO knife

Ruler

Pencil

Self-healing cutting mat

4 pieces of tape adhesive, 5⅛ in/12.5 cm long and ¼ in/6 mm wide

Paper hole punch, with a ⅛-in/3-mm hole

→

HOW TO

1 Set aside one of the five paper envelopes. With the remaining four envelopes, cut straight across the flap, leaving a ¼-in/6-mm flap. Make the cuts using the X-ACTO knife, ruler, pencil, and self-healing cutting mat.

2 Build the Accordion Envelope Card from the bottom up: Arrange the four envelopes on the work surface, one atop the other in a row, opening-side up, with the openings at the top. Join the envelopes together by taping the shortened flap of one envelope to the bottom back side of another envelope, in this way: First cut a piece of tape that is roughly the length of the envelope flap. Then apply the piece of tape to the flap and the back sides of the envelopes. Repeat until all four envelopes are taped together. Add the fifth envelope to the top of the accordion using the same technique.

3 Using the hole punch, punch a hole in the point of the triangular flap of the top envelope, ¼ in/6 mm in from the tip of the flap. Insert the brad through the hole so the round piece is on the outside of the flap, then separate the legs of the brad and flatten them against the underside of the flap to secure the brad to the envelope.

4 Fill the five envelopes with special messages, mementos, and trinkets.

→

5 Fold up the envelopes, one against the other like an accordion, in this manner: Starting with the bottom/first envelope, fold it up, along the top, so the back of the first envelope faces the back of the second envelope. Next, fold the second envelope up, along the top, so the front faces the front of the third envelope. Repeat the folding pattern with the remaining envelopes until they are stacked atop each other and can be tucked under the top/fifth envelope's flap.

6 Wrap the cotton ribbon around the closed accordion envelope card. To secure the ribbon, wrap the ends around the brad several times.

VARIATIONS

- Envelopes come in a variety of sizes, materials, and shapes, offering endless possibilities for creating different types of accordion envelope cards.

- Create patterned envelopes by imprinting shapes and motifs using a rubber stamp and a stamp pad.

ombré valentine

This Ombré Valentine conveys a simple and sweet message to a loved one. The recipient will not only enjoy the minimalist design and graded shades of pink, but will surely hang it on their wall as a reminder of your love. You can keep the white space blank or fill it up with photographs, drawings, or sweet messages.

MATERIALS

Ombré Valentine printable, one page

1 sheet of white cardstock, 8½ by 11 in/21.5 by 28 cm

1 piece of twine, 12 in/30.5 cm long

TOOLS

Computer and printer

X-ACTO knife

Ruler

Self-healing cutting mat

Paper hole punch, with ⅛-in/3-mm hole

HOW TO

1 With your computer, download this project's printable from www.chroniclebooks.com/bemine.

2 Print the Ombré Valentine printable onto the white cardstock.

3 Using the X-ACTO knife, ruler, and self-healing cutting mat, cut out the three components of the printable—"I," "Love," and "You"—so you have three separate cards.

→

I

LOVE

YOU

Using the paper hole punch, punch a hole in the two top corners of each card where there are small circles.

Stack the three cards so the holes are aligned and the words "I" and "Love" and "You" are visible. Thread the twine through the holes, starting and ending on the underside of the cards. Secure the ends with a knot.

VARIATIONS
- For a translucent effect, print the printable on clear vellum paper.
- Instead of twine, use ribbon or yarn.

stitched felt heart bag

Translucent glassine bags are one of my favorite supplies to use when packaging gifts. You can create visual interest with a sweet little felt heart and a personalized felt tag. Stitching up the top of the bag also gives the package a special detail. Flat felt works best for this project, but you could also use colored cardstock.

MATERIALS

1 piece of red felt,
1½ by 1½ in/4 by 4 cm

1 piece of white felt,
1 by 7 in/2.5 by 17.5 cm

1 glassine bag,
4½ by 6¾ in/11 by 17 cm

1 piece of red cotton thread,
8 in/20 cm long if using a sewing needle (or on a spool if using a sewing machine)

TOOLS

Scissors

Alphabet letter stamps, with letters that are no taller than ¼ in/6 mm

Stamp pad with fabric ink

Sewing needle (or sewing machine)

HOW TO

1 Using the scissors, fold the red felt piece in half and cut a 1-in-/2.5-cm-tall heart out of it.

→

2 Imprint a message onto the white felt using alphabet letter stamps and a fabric stamp pad. Using the scissors, cut out the message, creating a tag.

3 Place the candies or treats inside the glassine bag. Fold over the top of the bag two times.

4 Thread the sewing needle (or a sewing machine) with the red thread. Fold the white felt tag in half and place over the top edge of the bag so that 3½ in/9 cm of the tag is hanging down the front side of the bag. Stack the red heart on top of the white tag toward the top of the bag. Holding them in place, sew a running stitch across the top edge of the envelope about ¼ in/6 mm from the top edge, sewing over the heart and tag to secure them.

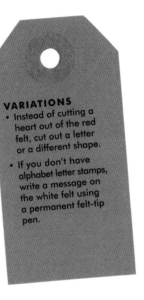

VARIATIONS
- Instead of cutting a heart out of the red felt, cut out a letter or a different shape.
- If you don't have alphabet letter stamps, write a message on the white felt using a permanent felt-tip pen.

love banner

A little handmade banner is a wonderful alternative to a traditional card. With a message like "I Love You," the banner can be hung by the recipient in their home to enjoy the message of love all year long. Rice paper is a beautiful thin, textured paper that can be found in art supply or paper stores, but you can also use any handmade paper or lightweight watercolor paper.

MATERIALS

Love Banner printable, three pages: Message Option 1, Message Option 2, Message Option 3

1 piece of rice paper, 4¼ by 5½ in/ 10.5 by 14 cm (or the paper of your choice)

1 wooden dowel, 5¼ in/13 cm long and ⅙ in/4 mm in diameter

1 piece of twine, 10 in/25 cm long

TOOLS

Computer and printer

Self-healing cutting mat

X-ACTO knife

Ruler

Glue stick

Scissors

HOW TO

1 With your computer, download this project's printable from www.chroniclebooks.com/bemine.

→

2 Choose the love banner printable you want to use for the project—either Message 1 ("I Love You"), Message 2 ("Je T'aime"), or Message 3 ("Te Amo"). Print that banner printable onto the rice paper.

3 Place the rice paper on the self-healing cutting mat and use the X-ACTO knife and ruler to cut out the banner, cutting neatly inside the black lines.

4 Place the banner on your work surface, right-side down, and using the glue stick, apply a ¾-in-/2-cm-wide strip of glue across the top of the banner. Wrap the glue-covered top of the banner around the center of the wooden dowel and hold it in place for 2 minutes. Let dry for 30 minutes.

5 Tie one end of the piece of twine to one end of the dowel at the edge of the banner and secure it with a knot. Tie the other end of the piece of twine to the other end of the dowel at the edge of the banner and secure it with a knot. Trim the ends of the twine with the scissors.

VARIATIONS
• Print the banner onto a printable fabric sheet. Printable fabric sheets are designed to be used for home printers and are available at your local craft store.
• Instead of wooden dowels, use colorful patterned paper straws.

yarn heart gift topper

I love creating gift toppers that the recipient can reuse or keep as decoration. This heart is fun to make and a great way to use up your yarn and cardboard scraps. You can attach the yarn heart to the top of a gift with adhesive or tie it around the gift with a length of yarn.

MATERIALS

Small scrap piece of cardboard
1 piece of yarn, 120 in/305 cm long
1 piece of glitter twine, 36 in/91 cm long

TOOLS

Scissors
Craft glue

HOW TO

1 Using the scissors, cut a circle with a 2½ in/6 cm diameter out of the cardboard.

2 Fold the cardboard circle in half, and in the middle of the half circle, cut out one-half of a heart shape. When you unfold the cardboard circle, you should have a hole in the shape of a heart in the center.

→

3 Place one end of the length of yarn at the top center of the heart and wrap it around once. Continue wrapping it around the cardboard shape, in through the inner hole and back out, again and again, adding loops in a clockwise direction until the whole cardboard surface is covered with yarn. Hide the ends of the yarn by tucking them under the loops on the back of the yarn-covered shape.

4 Place one end of the length of glitter twine at the top center of the yarn-covered shape. Start wrapping it around the yarn-covered shape as you did with the yarn, spacing the loops at ½-in/12-mm intervals. When you have wound the glitter twine around the whole yarn-covered shape, hide the ends by tucking them under the yarn loops on the back.

5 Affix the Yarn Heart Gift Topper to a wrapped gift using craft glue. Or, loop a piece of yarn through its center and tie it around the gift.

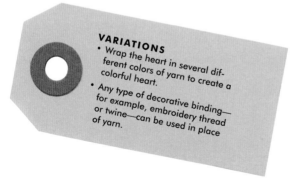

VARIATIONS
• Wrap the heart in several different colors of yarn to create a colorful heart.
• Any type of decorative binding—for example, embroidery thread or twine—can be used in place of yarn.

xoxox pop-up card

It's amazing all the interesting things you can create with paper and an X-ACTO knife. This XOXOX Pop-Up Card has a fun 3-D effect with a message that pops out at the recipient.

MATERIALS

XOXOX Pop-Up Card printable, one page

1 sheet of colored text-weight paper, 8½ by 11 in/21.5 by 28 cm

2 pieces of wood veneer paper, 4¼ by 5½ in/10.5 by 14 cm

Washi tape

TOOLS

Computer and printer

Self-healing cutting mat

Scissors

Ruler

X-ACTO knife

Bone folder

Clear double-sided tape

HOW TO

1 With your computer, download this project's printable from www.chroniclebooks.com/bemine.

2 Print the XOXOX Pop-Up Card printable onto the colored text-weight paper.

3 Place the wood veneer paper on the self-healing cutting mat. Stack the two pieces of wood veneer paper so the wood veneer surfaces face each other and all edges are aligned.

4 Using the scissors and the ruler, cut a 5½ in/14 cm length of washi tape. Place the washi tape

→

along a long edge of the stacked wood veneer paper, so half is on the paper and half is on the self-healing cutting mat. Fold the washi tape over so the two pieces of wood veneer become joined. Set the wood veneer card aside.

5 Using the X-ACTO knife, ruler, and self-healing cutting mat, cut out one of the XOXOX designs, cutting along the edges of the solid X and O shapes.

6 Using the bone folder and the self-healing cutting mat, score along the dashed lines that run vertically through the center of each X and O. Fold along the

scored lines so the XOXOX folds into an accordion shape.

7 Inside the wood veneer card, position the folded XOXOX accordion shape so the message will unfold and pop out when the card is opened. Using pieces of the double-sided tape, secure each end of the XOXOX design onto the interior surfaces of the card by taping down the outer legs of the Xs.

VARIATIONS
• Make the card out of colored card-stock instead of wood veneer.
• Print the XOXOX designs onto a sheet of patterned paper or glitter paper instead of colored text-weight paper.

i give you my heart card

One of my favorite things about making handmade cards is the aesthetic interest you can create by adding layers. Incorporating a 3-D focal point can make a card really pop. In this project, the glitter heart not only symbolizes love, but also adds engaging texture and dimension. Everyone loves keeping photograph cards, so this card is surely destined for display on the recipient's fridge or pin board.

MATERIALS

1 piece of glitter paper, 2 by 2 in/5 by 5 cm

1 piece of cardstock (in any color), 2 by 2 in/5 by 5 cm

One 3-D adhesive foam square, ½ in/12 mm square and ⅙ in/4 mm thick

1 photograph (4 by 5¼ in/10 by 13 cm) featuring a person holding out their hands

1 piece of colored cardstock, 4¼ by 5½ in/10.5 by 14 cm

TOOLS

1 heart paper punch, with 1½-in/4-cm heart hole

Glue stick

HOW TO

1 Using the heart paper punch, punch out one heart from the glitter paper and one heart from the 2-by-2-in/5-by-5-cm piece of cardstock. With the glue stick, glue the glitter heart onto the cardstock heart. Let dry for 5 minutes.

→

2 Remove the backing from one side of the foam square and adhere the foam square to the cardstock side of the glitter heart. Remove the backing from the other side of the foam square and position the glitter heart between the hands on the photograph. Press the glitter heart onto the photograph.

3 Using the glue stick, apply glue to the underside of the photograph and adhere it, centered, to the piece of colored cardstock.

VARIATIONS
• Write out a message on the plain heart cardstock and adhere it to the photograph instead of the glitter heart.
• If you don't have an adhesive foam square, glue together several small ½-in/12-mm squares of cardstock until the total thickness is ⅙ in/4 mm. Glue one side to the glitter heart and one side of the cardstock square to the photograph.

custom candy wrapper

Who doesn't love a sweet treat? Repackaging a candy bar can turn an ordinary treat into a special gift. The recipient will love the pretty presentation and heartfelt message. Custom-wrapped candy bars also make great party or wedding favors. This project is designed for candy bars that have been wrapped with foil and have a removable paper label.

MATERIALS

Custom Candy Wrapper printable, two pages: Patterned Paper and Message Labels

2 sheets of white sticker paper, 8½ by 11 in/21.5 by 28 cm

Foil-wrapped candy bar with paper label

TOOLS

Computer and printer

Ruler

Pencil

Piece of scrap paper

X-ACTO knife

Self-healing cutting mat

HOW TO

1 With your computer, download this project's printable from www.chroniclebooks.com/bemine.

→

2 Print out both pages (Patterned Paper and Message Labels) onto the front of the two sheets of white sticker paper.

3 Without disturbing the foil covering of the candy bar, remove the paper label. With the ruler, measure the length and width of the paper label. Make a note of the dimensions on the scrap paper.

4 Mark the patterned paper with the dimensions of the candy bar's original paper label and draw lines to connect the marks. Using the X-ACTO knife, ruler, and self-healing cutting mat, cut the patterned paper along the lines, so the cutout piece of the patterned paper matches the size of the original paper label.

5 Remove the sticker backing from the patterned paper. Wrap the patterned paper around the foil-wrapped candy bar, adhering it to the foil where the original paper label used to be.

6 Choose a message label for your customized candy bar from the Message Label printable—either "Happy [Heart] Day!" or "XOXO." Using the X-ACTO knife, ruler, and self-healing cutting mat, cut out the message label and remove the sticker backing. Wrap the message label around the left end of the candy bar, from the back to the front, so the message appears horizontally across the top surface of the candy bar.

VARIATIONS
- Instead of using one of the message labels from the printable, adhere letter stickers to the patterned paper wrapper, creating your own message.
- If you don't have sticker paper, print the printables onto white copy paper and use glue to adhere the patterned paper wrapper and message label.

crepe paper flower card

Flowers are a traditional symbol of love and affection. Create a petite crepe paper flower that will last forever. You can make one crepe paper flower to attach to a card or a small bouquet of flowers. The crepe paper flower can be reused for decoration or as a cake topper.

MATERIALS

1 piece of pink crepe paper,
6 by 6 in/15 by 15 cm

1 piece of green crepe paper,
2 by 2 in/5 by 5 cm

1 piece of green floral stem wire,
2½ in/6 cm long

1 piece of white cardstock,
4 by 5¼ in/10 by 13 cm

1 piece of washi tape,
4 in/10 cm long

1 piece of colored cardstock,
4¼ by 5½ in/10.5 by 14 cm

TOOLS

Scissors

Pencil

Ruler

Craft glue

Self-healing cutting mat

Screw punch, with ⅙-in/4-mm bit

Double-sided tape

→

HOW TO

1 Using the scissors, cut out 14 teardrop-shaped petals that are ¾ in/2 cm tall and ½ in/12 mm wide from the pink crepe paper. (Make sure you are cutting in the same direction as the crinkles in the crepe paper so you will be able to stretch out the petals.) From the green crepe paper, cut out two leaves that are ½ in/12 mm tall and ⅓ in/8 mm wide.

2 Using your thumbs, stretch out one of the pink crepe paper pieces into a cupped shape, so it resembles a flower petal. Repeat, with the remaining 13 flower petals.

3 Dab the bottom of one flower petal with a bit of craft glue and secure it to one end of the floral wire by twisting it around the wire. Repeat with the remaining flower petals, staggering the placement so the petals overlap, going down the wire, and open up like a flower. Put a dab of glue on the bottom of one green leaf and attach it to the wire at the bottom of the pink flower. Repeat, with the remaining green leaf. Set aside and let dry for 20 minutes.

4 Lay the white cardstock vertically on the self-healing cutting mat. Adhere the strip of washi tape horizontally across the bottom half of the front of the card. With the pencil and ruler, mark two holes 1 in/2.5 cm in from the left edge of the cardstock that are vertically aligned with ¾ in/2 cm of space between them. Using the screw punch, punch out the two holes.

5 Insert the floral wire stem through the holes in the white cardstock, entering down from the front through the top hole and up from the back side through the bottom hole, to secure the paper flower to the card.

6 Apply strips of double-sided tape to the back side of the white cardstock. Center the white cardstock on the piece of colored cardstock and press down firmly to join them together.

VARIATIONS
- Create a flower out of felt instead of crepe paper (and skip the step that involves stretching out the petals).
- Use crepe paper in a variety of colors to create a multicolored flower.

resources

Although you can find many of the materials and tools used in this book at your local art and craft supply store, there are also numerous online sources that sell fun creative materials. Here is a list of my favorite brands and sources.

art and craft supplies

DICK BLICK ART MATERIALS
www.dickblick.com

EKSUCCESS BRANDS
www.eksuccessbrands.com
The EK Tools paper punches are my favorite.

JO-ANN FABRIC & CRAFT STORES
www.joann.com

MARTHA STEWART CRAFTS
www.marthastewartcrafts.com

MICHAELS
www.michaels.com

adhesives

SCOTCH GLUES
www.scotchbrand.com
Scotch Wrinkle-Free Glue Stick is my favorite glue stick to use on paper craft projects. It is acid-free and safe to use on photos. Scotch Quick-Drying Tacky Glue is also a favorite adhesive to use in projects where a fast drying time is important.

fonts

DAFONT
www.dafont.com

HOUSE INDUSTRIES
www.houseind.com

THE LEAGUE OF MOVEABLE TYPE
www.theleagueofmoveabletype.com

LOST TYPE
www.losttype.com

MY FONTS
www.myfonts.com

paper

PAPER MART
www.papermart.com
Paper, tissue paper, crepe paper, and vellum.

PAPER SOURCE
www.papersource.com
Paper in the prettiest colors with coordinating envelopes, wrapping paper, and boxes.

ribbon and trim

STUDIO CARTA
www.angelaliguori.com
Beautiful Italian ribbons and twine in a huge array of colors.

TWILLTAPE.COM
www.twilltape.com
Twill tape in a variety of colors and widths.

specialty supplies

AMPERSANDITY
www.ampersandity.com
Custom hand-lettered rubber stamps.

BESOTTED BRAND
www.besottedbrand.com
Custom rubber stamps, twine, and packaging supplies.

CLEAR BAGS
www.clearbags.com
Clear plastic bags in a wide array of sizes.

CUTE TAPE
www.cutetape.com
Washi tape heaven.

FRAMINGSUPPLIES.COM
www.framingsupplies.com
Scotch Adhesive Transfer Tape is my favorite tape adhesive because it is stronger than conventional double-sided tape and works well with paper projects.

KNOT AND BOW
www.knotandbow.com
Confetti, stickers, and pretty paper goods.

PURL SOHO
www.purlsoho.com
Felt, fabric, and sewing supplies.

SHOP SWEET LULU
www.shopsweetlulu.com
Party supply central: patterned paper straws, confetti, and heart-shaped balloons.

SPOONFLOWER
www.spoonflower.com
Create your own custom fabric or purchase one of their many designs.

ULINE
www.uline.com
Mailing tubes, glassine bags, and kraft paper.

XYRON
www.xyron.com
The Xyron 1.5-inch Sticker Maker is one of my favorite tools for transforming paper or fabric into stickers.

acknowledgments

I am thankful for the opportunity to write a second book with Chronicle Books. My editor for *Pretty Packages,* Lisa Tauber, introduced me to my first editor of *Be Mine,* Laura Lee Mattingly. Laura Lee was a wonderful source of encouragement and wisdom and helped me develop a unique vision for *Be Mine.* And it was a privilege to work with my editor Elizabeth Yarborough on the completion of *Be Mine.* Her feedback and guidance was invaluable in creating this book.

Thank you to all the wonderfully creative individuals whose work helped make this book a reality. Thank you to Max Wanger for the beautiful images that grace the pages of the book. A big thank-you to Anne Kenady for designing the book so that each page is a visual treat.

To my dear friends and family, this book is for you! Your love and support has been the inspiration for *Be Mine.* Without your encouragement, this book would have not been possible.

To my parents, Daniel and Jane Kim, who were my first creative mentors, thank you for instilling in me a love of making things with my hands. I look back at my childhood and see the creative influence you played in my life, and I am grateful to be able to pass along this love of creating to your grandsons.

To my fun-loving boys, Jeremiah and Judah, I am honored to be your mommy. The two of you brighten my day with your laughter and love of life. Your endless creative energy always inspires me.

To my wonderful husband, Sang, thank you for taking this book-writing journey with me again. You are my best friend and the person I can depend on most in this world. Thank you for showing me throughout the years that a handwritten note or letter is one of the greatest treasures in life.